Lobbying for Good

How Business Advocacy Can Accelerate the Delivery of a Sustainable Economy

T0331490

Paul Monaghan

Director, Up the Ethics

Web: http://uptheethics.com

Email: paul@uptheethics.com

Twitter: @PaulJMonaghan

Philip Monaghan

Founder & CEO, Infrangilis | resilience in practice

Web: http://www.infrangilis.org

Email: philipmonaghan@infrangilis.org

Twitter: @Infrangilis_ltd

First published in 2014 by Dō Sustainability

87 Lonsdale Road, Oxford OX2 7ET, UK

ISBN 978-1-910174-13-5 (eBook-ePub)
ISBN 978-1-910174-14-2 (eBook-PDF)
ISBN 978-1-910174-12-8 (Paperback)

A catalogue record for this title is available from the British Library.

Dō Sustainability strives for net positive social and environmental impact. See our sustainability policy at **www.dosustainability.com**.

Page design and typesetting by Alison Rayner
Cover by Becky Chilcott

For further information on Dō Sustainability, visit our website: **www.dosustainability.com**

DōShorts

Dō Sustainability is the publisher of **DōShorts**: short, high-value ebooks that distil sustainability best practice and business insights for busy, results-driven professionals. Each DōShort can be read in 90 minutes.

New and forthcoming DōShorts – stay up to date

We publish 3 to 5 new DōShorts each month. The best way to keep up to date? Sign up to our short, monthly newsletter. Go to **www.dosustainability.com/newsletter** to sign up to the Dō Newsletter. Some of our latest and forthcoming titles include:

- *Understanding G4: The Concise Guide to Next Generation Sustainability Reporting* Elaine Cohen
- *Leading Sustainable Innovation* Nick Coad & Paul Pritchard
- *Leadership for Sustainability and Change* Cynthia Scott & Tammy Esteves
- *The Social Licence to Operate: Your Management Framework for Complex Times* Leeora Black
- *Building a Sustainable Supply Chain* Gareth Kane
- *Management Systems for Sustainability: How to Successfully Connect Strategy and Action* Phil Cumming
- *Understanding Integrated Reporting: The Concise Guide to Integrated Thinking and the Future of Corporate Reporting* Carol Adams
- *Corporate Sustainability in India: A Practical Guide for Multinationals* Caroline Twigg
- *Networks for Sustainability: Harnessing People Power to Deliver Your Goals* Sarah Holloway

- *Making Sustainability Matter: How To Make Materiality Drive Profit, Strategy and Communications*   Dwayne Baraka

- *Creating a Sustainable Brand: A Guide to Growing the Sustainability Top Line*   Henk Campher

- *Cultivating System Change: A Practitioner's Companion*   Anna Birney

- *How Much Energy Does Your Building Use*   Liz Reason

Subscriptions

In addition to individual sales of our ebooks, we now offer subscriptions. Access 60+ ebooks for the price of 5 with a personal subscription to our full e-library. Institutional subscriptions are also available for your staff or students. Visit **www.dosustainability.com/books/subscriptions** or email **veruschka@dosustainability.com**

Write for us, or suggest a DōShort

Please visit **www.dosustainability.com** for our full publishing programme. If you don't find what you need, write for us! Or suggest a DōShort on our website. We look forward to hearing from you.

....

Abstract

THE BUSINESS CASE for corporate responsibility or sustainability will never be strong enough to support an isolated business in its competition against the unscrupulous. The progressive vanguard reaches a point where it can advance no further without rendering itself uncompetitive. That is, unless advocacy and public policy intervention change the rules and shift the bar for the allowable lowest common denominator. With the base reset, so is the bar of aspiration. New rules enable new behaviours, with players competing on a fairer, more sustainable footing. This groundbreaking book, *Lobbying for Good*, describes how far-sighted businesses are rebooting the game, throwing off cultural inhibitions and sticking their head above the parapet to advocate progressive legislative change. The next phase of corporate responsibility and sustainability is underway, and it is *Lobbying for Good*.

....

About the Authors

PAUL MONAGHAN AND PHILIP E. MONAGHAN are recognised sustainability experts who have worked separately across the private, public and civil society sectors. The brothers have come together for *Lobbying for Good* because they passionately believe that progressive public policy intervention and advocacy will be the 'next big thing' for corporate responsibility and sustainability.

Paul Monaghan was architect of much of the UK co-operative movement's ethical and environmental excellence for nearly two decades. This included the creation of world-class programmes of advocacy and progressive public policy intervention, as well as environmental management, ethical finance and sustainability reporting. He has worked across sectors as diverse as banking, food, pharmacy, funerals and travel. Paul established Up the Ethics in 2013 to help pioneers of corporate responsibility and sustainability to take the next steps and help precipitate much needed systematic change.

Philip E. Monaghan is CEO of Infrangilis, a research agency on the green economy. A key pillar of Infrangilis's work is advising on or instigating advocacy initiatives on smart governance for a more resilient world. Areas of focus include sustainable urbanisation (Local Water, World Urban Campaign), green consumerism (Consumer Product Red List), and responsible capital markets (Rating Sovereign Raters). Philip is a recognised leader with over 20 years of international experience as a sustainability strategist. Prior to launching Infrangilis, his career included half a decade with AccountAbility where he helped establish the NGO's global advocacy leadership on corporate governance standards, before which he learned his trade in the private sector with engineers the WSP Group. He is also author of the books *Hard to Make, Hard to Break* and *Sustainability in Austerity*.

Contents

Preface

ONE OF THE MOST UNSAVOURY CHARACTERS in Tolkien's *Lord of the Rings* trilogy is Grima Wormtongue, the adviser to King Theoden of Rohan. He whispers from the shadows into the ear of the decrepit ruler, urging self-interest and accommodation with evil. Such is the common perception of how business lobbyists conduct themselves within the labyrinth of government: peddlers of dark influence and maintainers of the status quo. The tobacco sector's 50-year conspiracy to resist regulation, the chemical industry's routine attempts to keep products of proven toxicity on the shelves and fossil fuel's wholesale corruption of politics across the globe are just three examples of why such a negative perception is, in part, warranted.

There is another side to the story. Examples of business and business leaders engaging with public policy and making a substantive, positive difference to people and the planet. In the nineteenth century it was Cadbury, Lever, Owen and Rowntree. In the twenty-first century it is Aviva, Co-operative Energy, Gates, IKEA, Khosla, Maersk Line, Mooro, Skoll, Unilever and a host of others.

Lobbying for Good and its authors are not arguing that the glass is half full – the likes of the US Chamber of Commerce and BusinessEurope still wield far too much negative influence. But we are suggesting that there is a small and growing group of companies and business associations that have come to the conclusion that public policy intervention is an essential component of the transition to a more sustainable economy. We see this not only as a positive development, but as an absolute requirement for the world to have a cat in hell's chance of reinvigorating serious progress on issues such as climate change mitigation and trade justice. Moreover, we believe that most NGOs have reached the same conclusion as well.

As individuals, the authors have travelled different paths to reach the common conclusions of *Lobbying for Good*. We have been close to the small, but important breakthroughs that have nudged the agenda forward over the last two decades – such as the flagship interventions of AccountAbility and SustainAbility in 2005 (page 27). We have worked within and led advocacy campaigns for both business and NGOs – some of which were raging successes; others, abject failures. We have separately sat in meetings with the best and worst the business world has to offer (and the NGO world for that matter) and seen business's unparalleled capacity to create and destroy value with its political patronage.

The choice of exemplars has been a subject of heated debate – so much so that that we had to move our progress meetings out of the pub at one point. There are no angels on this earth. So, as with any business case study, it will be possible to dig and find inconsistencies (we flag some ourselves in places), but we trust they are not too many or large. For those who want to get into the game, our conclusions condense as suggestions for a *Lobbying for Good* (L4G) Advocacy Strategy. They are practical (we hope) and broad in scope. There are important areas we would have liked to consider further (such as how one best interacts with a public ballot such as Proposition 23 in California), but in a book designed as a 90-minute read compromises are unfortunately necessary.

The logic of *Lobbying for Good* is such that it is increasingly overriding the cultural aversion that rails against it, compelling business to act. Getting on board puts you not only in the company of some fantastic business leaders down the ages, but on the right side of history.

CHAPTER 1

Introduction

The inconvenient truth

'LEGISLATIVE INTERVENTION' is considered to be uniformly negative by most in the corporate word. Pejoratives abound: red-tape, bureaucracy, anti-business or granny state. The uncomfortable truth for those working in corporate responsibility and sustainability is that the vast bulk of progressive business conduct is driven by legislative intervention. Of course, there are corporate leaders who break away from the pack and go further than the norm, and these are vitally important as they demonstrate what is feasible. Yet it is legislation, and legislation alone, that has the ability to push an entire sector over into a new reality of business operation.

> ### The lobby – where the action is
> The historical roots of the term 'lobby' can be sourced back as far as 1640 and refer to the place where the British public would go to speak to their Member of the House of Commons. The United States has its own mythology of the origination of the term – tracking it back to the nineteenth century and the pestering of President Grant in the reception of the Willard Hotel by 'those damn lobbyists'.

For the purposes of *Lobbying for Good* we will focus on businesses (and their intermediaries) who seek to persuade a public official (elected or unelected) to take a preferred route to regulation, legislation and budgeting.

We will also look at broader issues of advocacy, whereby a business seeks to effect political change more indirectly – perhaps seeking to influence the opinion of the public, media, trade associations or other target audiences, so that they may in turn influence public policy.

Far-sighted businesses know public policy intervention is key to sector change, and are now throwing off cultural inhibitions and sticking their head above the parapet to advocate progressive legislative change. They know that the 'business case' for corporate responsibility or sustainability will never be strong enough to support an isolated business in its competition against the unscrupulous. They understand that the progressive vanguard reaches a point where it can advance no further without rendering itself uncompetitive. That is, unless advocacy and public policy intervention changes the rules and shifts the bar for the allowable lowest common denominator. With the base reset, so is the bar of aspiration. New rules enable new behaviours, with players competing on a fairer, more sustainable footing.

Consider the pressures driving a stock-market listed European food retailer to improve the environmental performance of their operations – let us call them Progressive Up To A Point plc, or PUTAP. Yes, there will be small amounts of pressure from PUTAP's investors urging them to keep their brand clear of scandal and not come across as an environmental laggard. Yes, a small percentage of consumers will vote with their feet and go out of their way to shop there if they go the extra mile and communicate it well. Yes, PUTAP may find it can better attract that minority of the workforce who rate a clean conscience over the size of their wage packet.

However, it is the EU Waste Framework Directive (perhaps supplemented by a national Landfill Tax) and the EU Packaging Directive that will have largely driven massive improvements in PUTAP's recycling and waste minimisation over the last decade. It is almost certain that the F-gas regulations of 2006 forced them to phase out potent ozone depletors such as CFCs and HCFCs from their refrigeration systems. It was the EU's Directive of 1998 which ensured that PUTAP's transport fleet could no longer pump toxic lead into the atmosphere. The same story is unfolding across many other parts of the world. In the United States it will have been the numerous iterations of the Clean Air Act that has successfully driven improvements in pollution connected to power plant and transport (and thus tackled contributions to acid rain, smog and mercury and nitrogen deposition). In Japan, the Receptacle Packaging Recycle Law of 1997 and the Fundamental Law for Establishing a Sound Material-Cycle Society of 2000 have entrenched producer responsibility of waste and helped the country become a global leader in recovery and recycling. Moreover, once legislatively driven change has been embedded across a sector it rarely reverts backward to what was the dirty norm – it would take a brave corporate indeed to argue for the reintroduction of lead to petrol or CFCs to coolants. Legislatively driven change reboots the system and creates a new baseline. The wheels of commerce keep turning as before. Profits continue to flow. The world moves on. Things are better.

Of course, there will be times when such environmental legislation is amended or even reversed; times when legislation is badly crafted and hinders instead of helps. But these are the exception. There is an overpowering trend in both developed and emerging economies for incremental platforms of environmental legislation (much as there is for health and safety and labour standards) and for these to enjoy broad public support. Those who call for bonfires of red-tape will ultimately have as much long-term success as Guy Fawkes and his gunpowder plot – they swim against not just the tide of history, but the wishes of the majority of humanity.

Right across the world, people are calling for increased government regulation. Edelman's polling of 'informed publics' (**http://www.edelman. com/insights/intellectual-property/2014-edelman-trust-barometer/ about-trust/global-results/**) in 2013 found a three-to-one margin of support for increased government regulation of the financial services, energy and food and beverage industries. Delving deeper: in Germany 66% said that there was not enough regulation of the financial services industry; in the UK 73% said the same of the energy industry; and in China 84% said that there was not enough regulation of the food and beverage industry. The likes of the US Chamber of Commerce and BusinessEurope, for all their legion of short-sighted and irresponsible influences, appear to have little real legitimacy and are very much on the wrong side of history.

Pioneers of *Lobbying for Good*

Past leaders who have championed corporate responsibility are often viewed through the crude lens of philanthropy and how much wealth they donated. Yet the truly great business leaders throughout history have always grasped that legislative intervention can be a force for good.

LOBBYING FOR GOOD: HOW BUSINESS ADVOCACY CAN ACCELERATE THE DELIVERY OF A SUSTAINABLE ECONOMY

The timeline depicted in Figure 1 lists some of the key events that have shaped interest or action in corporate lobbying over the past 400 years (events that are explored further throughout this chapter).

In the nineteenth century the UK wrestled with the enormous opportunities and problems brought by industrialisation and accelerated urbanisation. The political establishment was packed with landed gentry keen on protecting their age old rights and privileges, and there was also an emergent self-made business class seeking to press selfish interests of its own. However, there were also those who saw not just profit opportunities, but how the world might be a better place.

At the turn of the century, Robert Owen was pioneering enlightened new work practices at his New Lanark cotton mill in Scotland, including the introduction of the world's first infant school. But he was also 'fathering' the world's co-operative enterprise movement (page 43), which now has over a billion members, and spent the greater part of his adult life lobbying for the reform of working conditions. Similarly, at the latter end of the century, William Lever's creation of the Port Sunlight garden village to house his company's workers attracted attention the world over, and his businesses went on to form one of the world's first multinational companies, Unilever (page 29). But he was also a Member of Parliament who in his maiden speech called for the state to have a role in the provision of pensions, and later went on to introduce a private members' bill on the issue. And the list goes on. John Cadbury brought chocolate to the masses, and in his spare time campaigned against the use of young boys as chimney sweeps and helped establish the forerunner to the Royal Society for the Prevention of Cruelty to Animals, which is today the world's largest animal welfare charity. Joseph Rowntree, another successful chocolatier, made sure that not all of the trusts he established were charitable as he wanted them to be able to 'search out the underlying causes' of social ills and if necessary seek to 'change the laws of the land'.

....

FIGURE 1. Timeline of milestones in corporate lobbying.

1600s	1800s	1970s	1980s	1990s	2000s	Present day
Public said to lobby politicians for the first time in UK House of Commons	Rise of global-isation and emer-gence of modern CR (e.g. Ben & Jerry's, The Body Shop)		'Cash for questions' scandal and new forms of regula-tion (e.g. US Lobbying Disclosure Act; UK Com-mittee on Standards in Public Life).			Resurgence in advocacy and *Lobby-ing for Good* (e.g. B-Corps, Unilever). European Transparen-cy Register comes into effect.
	Industrial revolution and first wave of *Lobby-ing for Good* (e.g. Owen, Lever, Cadbury)		'Tuna-gate' affair and early form of regula-tion (e.g. Canada Lobbyist Registra-tion Act)		'Influencing Power' and 'Towards Responsible Lobbying' urge CR community to take ac-tion. GRI G3 asks for dis-closure of public policy & political donations	

SOURCE: Up the Ethics and Infrangilis, 2014.

....

LOBBYING FOR GOOD: HOW BUSINESS ADVOCACY CAN
ACCELERATE THE DELIVERY OF A SUSTAINABLE ECONOMY

Across the Atlantic, the United States had a different tradition. Famous philanthropists such as Andrew Carnegie, John Rockefeller and John Pierpont Morgan certainly left large charitable legacies, but their approach to business conduct was much less progressive. So much so, they were ignominiously labelled as 'robber barons'. Andrew Carnegie, the 'patron saint of libraries' was comfortable using an armed private militia to break up a strike at one of his steel mills. John Rockefeller famously became the 'world's richest man', and his funding helped eradicate hookworm and yellow fever, but the business practices of his oil operations were such that antimonopoly legislation was introduced and eventually led to Standard Oil being dissolved. JP Morgan was both a prominent banker and supporter of the arts, but another who saw business holdings declared illegal under antitrust law.

In contrast, many of North America's technology and dot-com business pioneers have an appetite for both philanthropy and *Lobbying for Good*. Bill Gates, the co-founder of Microsoft, is applauded for the generosity of his charitable donations and their impact on poverty alleviation in the developing world, which now amount to an incredible US$28 billion. Less well known is how politically active he is. Gates provided time, energy and money to the UK's 'IF Campaign' in 2013, which sought to influence that year's G8 meeting in Northern Ireland to focus on a basket of policy asks to 'make poverty history'. A close look at the Bill and Melinda Gates Foundation also reveals a strong 'policy and advocacy' programme. Some US$134 million has been spent in support of tobacco control and measures such as indoor smoking bans and tobacco taxes. Jeff Skoll, co-founder of eBay, the world's largest online marketplace, has given over half of his fortune away and contributed US$1 billion to his Foundation. He also founded Participant Media, which backs feature films and documentaries that 'inspire and accelerate social change' and, crucially, builds 'social action and advocacy campaigns' alongside them. Participant Media were major backers of influential movies such as *An Inconvenient Truth*, *Darfur Now*, *Food Inc*, *The Cove* and 40-plus other projects. Intel co-founder, Gordon Moore has established a Foundation with more than US$5 billion of assets and has a strong record of supporting environmental conservation. Moore also backed the campaign to successfully defend California's progressive environmental legislation with a US$1 million donation; and was joined in this by Sun Microsystems co-founder Vinod Khosla and Google co-founder Sergey Brin, who donated US$200,000.

Of course, it is easy to find inconsistencies and oddities in the activity of all of these pioneering business leaders – Owen's spiritualism, Gates's alleged blind spot on corporate tax avoidance and Lever's apparent comfort with slave labour at his palm oil plantations. None of them are a saint (who is?) but they have all made the world a better place with their *Lobbying for Good*.

Into the light

Ironically, whilst business is generally averse to government intervening in its affairs, it has no problem involving itself in the affairs of government. To many, corporate lobbying is the antithesis of corporate responsibility. They see it as a persistent block to the advancement of progressive social, ethical and environmental legislation. It is an assault on democracy; an evil to be fought. However, the legitimacy of corporates lobbying for change is long recognised. Not just legally (as in the constitution of the United States, which enshrines the right to petition government), but in the minds of people the world over. The aforementioned polling by Edelman (page 18) found that 79% of people across the world believe business should be involved in formulating regulation in industries such as energy and food.

Certainly there are numerous examples of corporate lobbying flying in the face of truth and spreading lies and falsehoods; of the democratic process being circumvented via bribes and threats. The foreword of *Towards Responsible Lobbying* suggests that it may even be the second-oldest profession on the planet. Hardly surprising when even late into the twentieth century bribes to foreign public officials were not only legal, but tax deductible in countries such as Australia, France, Germany and New Zealand.

In the late 1980s and early 1990s matters reached a nadir with a series of political scandals on both sides of the Atlantic. Canada had the 'Tunagate affair', the United States had the 'Wedtech scandal' and the United Kingdom had 'cash-for-questions' revelations. The scale of public outcry was such that governments were forced to take action, first in North America, and then in Europe. This increasing regulation of lobbying and political donations not only shows no signs of letting up, but has expanded into the related area of payments to government for access to natural resources.

Canada set the ball rolling with a Lobbyist Registration Act in 1988. Communications with any employee of 'Her Majesty in Right of Canada' now attract a registration obligation to those who operate professionally. They were followed by the United States and the Lobbying Disclosure Act of 1995 that required lobbyists to file activity reports and allow the public to know who was being paid how much to lobby whom on what. Amendments to both Acts have followed, and loopholes that allow lobbying activity to be channelled through third parties such as the US Chamber of Commerce (who were the single largest outside spender in the 2010 elections) are currently under scrutiny from the Securities and Exchange Commission. It is interesting to speculate whether the progressive decline in US lobbying spend since 2010 is a consequence of the economic downturn or the chill wind of lobbyist regulation and lobbying disclosure.

In the United Kingdom, in 1994 a Committee on Standards in Public Life was established and longstanding requirements for business to disclose political donations were augmented with a ban on Members of Parliament tabling questions and amendments on behalf of outside interests. The UK is presently advancing a Lobbying Act that not only introduces a statutory register of consultant lobbyists but, controversially, regulates more closely the spending of NGOs in the run up to elections.

The European Union launched a 'Transparency Initiative' in 2005, and now operates a system of carrots and sticks to persuade 'interest representatives' to sign up to its voluntary Transparency Register, such as facilitated access to premises. In 2014, the European Parliament called on the Commission to make the lobby register mandatory by 2017. In a related development, in 2013, Europe signed into law new requirements for the extractive and forestry industries to disclose all payments over €100,000 made to governments on a country-by-country and project-by-project basis. This mirrors similar requirements in the US for oil and mining companies reporting to the Securities and Exchange Commission that are under consideration; and pending reporting standards in Canada.

Such concern is not restricted to the Northern Hemisphere either. Polling (**http://ec.europa.eu/public_opinion/flash/fl_363_sum_en.pdf**) in Brazil and India has found that in 2012 21% and 27% of the public respectively state that 'excessive influence on government policy' was one of the 'main negative effects of companies on society'. The United States topped the concern levels with 38%, followed by Europe with 28%. Only in China did it appear people were relaxed, with just 9% concerned about undue influence.

Investigative journalism has played a big part in uncovering corruption and driving improved standards, but so has the emergence of campaign groups that focus on corporate corruption and excess. Globally, there are big hitters like Transparency International, which now has more than one hundred chapters across the world. There is also Avaaz, which in 2014 prioritised 'fighting political corruption, including corporate capture of our governments' following a poll of its 34 million members. More locally, there are highly effective groups such as Public Citizen in the United States and the Alliance for Lobbying Transparency and Ethics Regulation (ALTER-EU) in Europe, which have an uncanny ability to home in and uncover abuses.

The increasing requirements for lobbyists to behave better and be more transparent look set to continue; not least because lobbyists are themselves in favour of more regulation as they know they have an image problem (to put it mildly). As never before, it is now necessary for progressive businesses to ensure that there are no major lobbying disconnects in their operations. Progress to date is patchy: just 30% of the 1,700 businesses who responded to the UN Global Compact's 'Annual Implementation Survey' (**http://www.**

unglobalcompact.org/docs/issues_doc/Environment/climate/Guide_
Responsible_Corporate_Engagement_Climate_Policy.pdf) say that they
have 'Aligned traditional government affairs activities (i.e., lobbying)
with corporate responsibility commitments'; although 60% do claim to
'Publically advocate for action in relation to the Global Compact principles
and/or other UN goals.' As the United Nations Secretary-General said
when addressing business leaders at a Global Compact Summit:
'Business must restrain itself from taking away, by its lobbying activities,
what it offers through corporate responsibility and philanthropy.'

Yet, as welcome as the removal of inconsistency and hypocrisy would
be, there is a much more exciting additional dimension to this issue.
Can a business's lobbying be pro-actively deployed to do good? Could
business advocacy not only be a centrepiece of corporate responsibility
programmes, but a game-changing new means for the realisation of
sustainable development?

In the next chapter we will see how a generation of New Pioneers are
rebooting the game, throwing off cultural inhibitions and advocating
progressive legislative change. The next phase of corporate responsibility
and sustainability is underway, and it is *Lobbying for Good*.

....

CHAPTER 2

The New Pioneers

ALONE AND WITH OTHERS. Big and small. Business will always lobby for change, what we need now is a lot more *Lobbying for Good*. Rightly or wrongly; business support and policy endorsements carry great weight with politicians and regulators. They are particularly valued when they relate to the economic costs and benefits of policy options.

In 2005, two flagship publications called on corporate responsibility and sustainability professionals to stop turning a blind eye to the lobbying that was going on under their noses and to seek to draw it into the light. SustainAbility and WWF's *Influencing Power* (**http://www.sustainability.com/library/ influencing-power#.U3zBJP14wWZ**) found that whilst most of the world's largest companies struck an overwhelmingly defensive tone, approximately half provided at least some information on their lobbying. AccountAbility and the UNGC's *Towards Responsible Lobbying* (**http://www.accountability. org/about-us/publications/towards.html**) noted the increasing influence of the world's 100,000-plus lobbyists, and proposed a framework to identify the degree to which activities were being pursued responsibly. Whilst each painted a depressing picture at times, both also envisaged the possibility of lobbying driving stronger social and environmental policy frameworks in support of core business activities – and that is exactly what has emerged over the ensuing decade amongst a cadre of progressive New Pioneers.

In *Lobbying for Good*, we bring the state of play up to date, but also set out practical suggestions for how businesses can set about engaging for change, via a *Lobbying for Good* (L4G) Advocacy Strategy.

In this chapter we will look at how organisations of all types are impacting public policy in positive ways, as illustrated in Figure 2. We begin with how big multinational businesses such as Unilever and IKEA are mobilising their big machines to advocate for sustainable development in support of their business strategies. We then look at how multinationals such Aviva and Maersk Line have sought to join together with others for a cause and pursued strength in numbers. Lastly, we see how mid-corporates such as Co-operative Energy and collaborations of smaller businesses such as the Main Street Alliance are showing that organisations of all sizes can impact public policy, for the good of themselves and society.

FIGURE 2. Organisations of all types impacting on public policy in positive ways.

Mid-corporates and small business driving change
Co-operative Energy & 'Community Renewables and Market Diversity'
American Sustainable Business Council & 'Fair Minimum Wage'

Joining together for a cause
AVIVA & 'Corporate Sustainability Reporting Coalition'
Maersk Line & 'Sustainable Shipping Initiative'
Alliance Boots & 'Circular Economy Task Force'

Big business mobilising their big machines
Unilever 'Sustainable Living Plan'
IKEA 'People and Planet Positive'

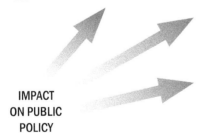

IMPACT
ON PUBLIC
POLICY

SOURCE: Up the Ethics and Infrangilis, 2014.

Big business mobilising their big machines

Unilever

By any measure Unilever is big. Its products are sold in 190 countries and generated sales of €50 billion in 2013. They proudly claim that 'More than two billion consumers use a Unilever product on any given day.' Late in 2010, they set out a bold Sustainable Living Plan that pledged, over ten years, to halve the environmental footprint of their products whilst helping one billion people improve their health and well-being – and all against a background vision to double the size of the business.

The accompanying press release emphasised continuity with the values of founding father William Lever, a nineteenth-century pioneer of progressive advocacy and political intervention (page 19). From the outset, CEO Paul Polman emphasised that for Unilever to achieve its goals the company would need to work in partnership not just with customers, suppliers and NGOs but also governments. Their website underscores the point and explains the rationale, saying: 'We need to actively engage with governments and regulators to create an environment that can help us achieve the commitments set out in the Unilever Sustainable Living Plan... Many of the impacts of our operations fall outside of our direct control as so we need to engage governments to create an environment that is supportive to meeting the big sustainability challenges the world faces. These range from local infrastructure that supports consumer recycling through to trade terms that support sustainably sourced agricultural commodities.' Essentially, they are arguing that the rules of the game need to be rebooted to ensure that it is profitable to 'do the right thing'. They have even gone so far as to argue (rightly) that corporate silence on issues such as climate change is not an abstention from the debate, but rather, 'an abdication of responsibility for which no amount of other corporate good deeds can compensate'. Interestingly, Unilever is keen to stress the safeguards they have in place to ensure that their lobbying activities meet some baseline standards. Their Code of Business Principles stipulates that they will not support political parties or fund groups that promote party interests. In Europe, they subscribe to the Code of Conduct for Public Affairs Professionals as developed by the Society for European Affairs Professionals, and are listed in the European Transparency Register.

Significantly, in 2011 they created an Advocacy team (now five-strong) with the aim of stepping up their engagement and 'working together with other stakeholders to bring about changes in public policy in key areas of health and sustainability'. Climate change, public health and waste were formally identified as the priority areas for policy intervention – although a reading of their engagement activity indicates international development and poverty alleviation are also key areas of activity. Unilever's willingness to engage has opened influential doors the world over. In 2011, CEO Paul Polman attended the business meeting of the G20 Heads of State and Government and presented an action plan on behalf of the B20 Working Group on Development and Food Security, of which he is co-chair. A year later, they were present at the United Nations Conference on Sustainable Development in Rio, and Polman was appointed to the UN High-level Panel of Eminent Persons on the Post-2015 Development Agenda.

Energetic globetrotting of this ilk is required in order to sway political discourse in a positive direction. As Thomas Lingard, Global Advocacy Director at Unilever, points out: 'Governments who try to change the rules will find all those who stand to lose out banging on their door, spelling out just how bad the consequences of that change will be for them, their supply chains, employees and the economy as a whole. The voices demanding the changes are not always so loud, especially where the industries that will benefit may not exist yet, as is the case with many of the new low carbon technology ventures that would reasonably be expected to prosper in a true low carbon economy.'

However, even a slick, committed pioneer can encounter a few bumps on the road – especially one that has acquired a challenger brand along the way.

The US ice cream maker Ben & Jerry's became a subsidiary in 2000, and from the outset Unilever and the Ben & Jerry's founders were keen to emphasise that not only would the cutting-edge ethics not be compromised, but they would be expected to permeate the parent group. They have remained true to their word, and even today the Ben & Jerry's brand champions issues many other corporates would shy away from. In 2012, an election year in the US, they supported a 'Get the Dough out of Politics' campaign to challenge the Supreme Court ruling of 2010 that companies should have the ability to spend unlimited amounts during election time. In a nice touch, founders Ben Cohen and Jerry Greenfield were heavily involved, as well as the current CEO, Jostein Solheim. Another issue they have been vocal on is mandatory labelling of genetically modified foods (GMOs) and the consumer's right to know, so much so that they are a part of 'Just Label It!', a national coalition of groups calling on the US Food and Drink Administration to require GMO labelling.

Bizarrely, in 2012 Unilever is reported to have contributed in excess of US$450,000 to defeat a Californian ballot in favour of GMO labelling –

and this resulted in some negative publicity and even boycott calls of Ben & Jerry's products. However, both the press coverage and boycott calls were muted and it would appear that Unilever's good works and honourable ambitions have granted the business a certain leeway to be inconsistent. This is welcome given many companies are paranoid about being one hundred percent aligned before they engage in *Lobbying for Good*. The vast majority of the public (and even large sections of the media) understand that the pursuit of perfection should never be allowed to become the enemy of progress.

IKEA

In early 2011, the relatively new Chief Sustainability Officer of IKEA, Dr Steve Howard, was asked about their appetite for public policy intervention. He admitted that to date there had been little activity as it had not been viewed as being part of their 'identity' but said that: 'We recognise that we need to be at the table and more part of the discussion. Things that are important to us like renewable-energy investments and public-transport infrastructure are always heavily reliant on public policy.'

Lo and behold, in late 2012 when IKEA launched its first Sustainability Strategy 'People and Planet Positive', advocacy was firmly recognised as a key element of delivery. It needed to be if the business was to be a sector leader given the Swedish home furnishings retailer has operations in 43 countries, offers a range of 9,500 products and had sales of €27.9 billion in 2013. The public policy engagements reported in their 2012 Sustainability Report were scant, amounting to little more than a list of memberships of trade associations. But the following year, impressive engagements were detailed in areas as diverse as climate change, waste, resource efficiency, forest management and chemicals. They supported proposals for reform of the EU Emissions Trading Scheme (so that it might better achieve its purpose of stimulating investment in low carbon technology); contributed to consultations on plastic waste policy and EU waste targets (calling for improved take-back schemes and incentives for consumers); wrote to the European Commission and Swedish Ministry of Environment (to encourage clearer definition of Endocrine Disruptor Chemicals and further opportunities for their restriction); contributed to the EC's 2030 Framework for Climate and Energy Policy (seeking policies that would favour long-term investments in renewable energy and the promotion of energy efficiency solutions) and liaised with various governments to help combat illegal logging.

The pace was maintained in the early part of 2014, when in February (along with Unilever) they wrote to the UK Secretary of State for Business, Innovation and Skills urging that the UK Government not seek to water down pending EU legislation requiring mandatory sustainability reporting by large business. In March, with 36 other organisations, they co-signed a letter to the EU Heads of State and Government urging them to stay strong and agree strong European greenhouse gas targets of at least 40% reduction by 2020. Not bad from a virtual standing start; and, encouragingly, IKEA's advisory group of external advisors are reported to want to see it doing even more.

Howard was previously CEO and co-founder of The Climate Group, and is both adept and passionate about anything and everything relating to reduced carbon emissions. Late in 2013, IKEA were a key supporter of a *Guide for Responsible Corporate Engagement in Climate Policy* (**http:// www.unglobalcompact.org/docs/issues_doc/Environment/climate/ Guide_Responsible_Corporate_Engagement_Climate_Policy.pdf**). This

Guide (which demonstrates how *Lobbying for Good* is entering the mainstream) sets out the rationale for companies to align their climate policy positions to their previously stated pronouncements on the subject. Production of the Guide was managed by UN Global Compact, who pointed out that just 30% of their members are currently demonstrating such alignment (page 25). At launch Howard commented: 'There is an old expression which is that winners go to market and losers go to Washington. But we now need the winners to go to Washington and Brussels and Beijing to help unlock businesses innovation and investment to get this problem solved... We cannot defend the status quo and at the same time build a sustainable future at pace and scale. The strategic assets of the 21st century will be clean air and clean water and renewable energy; it is not about defending the right to pollute.' The Guide was pointedly launched in the run up to the UN Climate Change Conference (COP19) in Warsaw. The Executive Director of the UNFCC, Christiana Figueres noting with concern that clean energy lobbying has to date been 'outgunned and outfinanced by fossil fuel lobbying', and that 'if we don't have a voice that is equally as orchestrated with arguments that are at least equally as compelling, then governments are going to be taking very timid decisions and they're not going to be tipping the scale'.

The big test will be UNFCC COP21 in Paris in 2015: will the newly found confidence of progressive businesses such as IKEA and Unilever be enough to counter the power and influence of the fossil fuel lobby? It needs to if there is to be the remotest chance of a binding international agreement emerging for greenhouse gas emissions.

Lessons in leadership
- The issues chosen need to be material to the business' operations and explainable – no ambulance chasing

- If you have it, 'heritage' is a great card to play – it can inspire employees

- Leadership can be built quickly if you enjoy good relations with NGOs – in fact, poaching a talented individual from an NGO might help enormously

- Integration of lobbying activity with sustainability reporting is essential – as with most things, sunlight is a great disinfectant (and it keeps you honest)

- Try to involve a CEO or other senior business leader at the front end of campaigns, and be bold – the world really does want to see more *Lobbying for Good*, and will forgive the odd inconsistency

Joining together for a cause – strength in numbers

ClimateWise

'As business leaders, you must make it clear to your leaders that doing the right thing for the climate is also the smart thing for global competitiveness and long-term prosperity.' So pleaded Ban Ki Moon, United Nations Secretary General in the run up to the clearly stalling Copenhagen round of climate change talks in 2009. One area of business that has heeded the call to arms more than any other is the insurance sector; they have been quick not only to grasp the enormity of the impact of climate change, but of the need to act. They understand that climate change is now increasing the frequency and severity of extreme weather events, and the situation will deteriorate further if left unchecked.

Economic losses caused by natural catastrophes are already on the rise – the Munich Re insurance group has calculated that weather-related losses and damage have increased from an annual average of US$50 billion in the 1980s to close to US$200 billion over the last decade. As early as 2007, the ClimateWise initiative was urging insurers not just to better understand and manage climate change, but to 'work with policy makers nationally and internationally to help them develop and maintain an economy that is resilient to climate risk'. It even advocated that they 'support work to set and achieve national and global emissions reduction targets' and they 'support Government action, including regulation, that will enhance the resilience and reduce the environmental impact of infrastructure and communities'. Some 40 insurers from across the world are now signed up, of which 27 disclose annually the degree to which they comply with the ClimateWise principles. The project is an exemplar of how a range of businesses in a sector can contribute individually and en masse to progressive policy development in an open and transparent manner.

Aviva & the Corporate Sustainability Reporting Coalition

One insurer that wanted to go further and faster than peers was Aviva, which has 31 million customers spread across 17 countries and £241 billion of funds under management. They can trace their history back more than three hundred years (to 1696) and have sought to maintain the capacity to think in the long term and identify emerging strategic risks.

In 2001 they became the first asset manager in the world to systematically vote against the Report and Accounts of companies that failed to disclose material sustainability information. However, they found that progress was painfully slow. At current rates, it would be decades before sustainability reporting was common practice across global markets – 75% of companies do not report on sustainability issues, limiting the ability of markets to integrate sustainability into company valuation. Legislative intervention was needed to drive meaningful change. As Steve Waygood, Chief Responsible Investment Officer at Aviva Investors, points out: 'Markets are driven by information. If the information the market receives is short term, then these characteristics will define the way these markets operate. It is time for regulators to act.'

In September 2011 Aviva convened the Corporate Sustainability Reporting Coalition (CSRC) with a view to realising rule change across the globe. The CSRC was an eclectic mix of pension funds, asset managers, church organisations, charities and professional bodies; that, crucially, had between them US$2 trillion of assets under management. They argued that there is a solid business case for regulatory intervention, saying: 'It has been demonstrated that there is a direct correlation between sustainable business practices and the longer-term financial success of that company. Disclosure is a powerful motivational management highlighting areas of underperformance that are important to the long-term health of the business. This will help capital to be allocated to more sustainable, responsible companies and strengthen the long-term sustainability of the financial system.'

Even such as powerful a coalition as this could not hope to trek across the globe and seek to persuade individual countries and their stock exchanges to take action. So, they looked towards an umbrella solution; and, in 2012, the CSRC took their message to the United Nations Rio+20 Earth Summit. Whilst disappointed not to secure backing for a global policy framework in the summit outcomes, they moved the issue forward by securing a paragraph recognising the importance of such reporting. This in turn led the governments of Brazil, Denmark, France and South Africa (all countries with some form of mandatory sustainability reporting already in place) to form 'The Group of Friends of Paragraph 47' – now joined by Austria, Colombia, Norway and Switzerland. In parallel developments, the UK government made great play at the Summit of the introduction of mandatory carbon footprint reporting for all firms listed on the Main Market of the London Stock Exchange (with Aviva, not coincidentally, part of the official UK delegation in Rio).

Aviva's Waygood believes that a number of factors were critical to the success at Rio: the breadth of CSRC's support provided legitimacy to the call for action; the involvement of Stakeholder Forum helped the coalition navigate the complex and nuanced workings of the United Nations; and Aviva's continued appetite for the issue was sustained by a series of CEOs who recognised its importance and allowed appropriate time, energy and resource to be allocated to the cause. In April 2014, the campaign secured another major win when the European Parliament agreed to back reforms that mandate large listed companies to report on their environmental and social impacts – a significant step given the wrong-headed opposition of business lobbyists such as BusinessEurope. The legislation may not be as extensive or detailed as some activists might have hoped, but it would never have progressed without the *Lobbying for Good* of Aviva and others.

Maersk Line & the Sustainable Shipping Initiative

Another multinational that has taken the bull by the horns is Maersk Line, the world's largest shipping company. A truly global operation, with

32,000 staff across 125 countries and US$26 billion of revenue; they were a founder member of the Sustainable Shipping Initiative (SSI) that was established by Forum for the Future in 2010. The SSI aims to ensure that the industry has both a profitable and sustainable future, and now includes 19 major businesses (such as ABN AMRO, Cargill and DNV), along with NGOs such as WWF. In 2011, the SSI issued *The Case for Action*, which identified key sustainability challenges for the industry. Later in the year, its members produced a response in *Vision for 2040*, and initiated workstreams on everything from greenhouse gas reduction targets through to new eco-ship designs. Crucially, a key pillar to delivery of *Vision for 2040* is the recognition that there needs to be sustainable governance of the oceans and this requires the development of better global standards and support for 'progressive legislation aimed at significantly improving social, environmental and economic sustainability across the shipping industry'.

Jacob Sterling, Head of Sustainability at Maersk Line, explains the rationale for helping establish the SSI campaign: 'The challenge of taking a sector lead on sustainable development is the competitive disadvantage it can lead to. Take the issue of sulphur oxides reduction: cleaner fuel is more expensive and fuel costs are a significant portion of total operating costs. This means acting alone is difficult. So we need regulation to make it work. We have voluntarily switched to a cleaner fuel in certain regions to show it is feasible, with mixed results. Hong Kong is committed to introducing higher standards in 2015. But in New Zealand we were forced to switch back to traditional fuels after a one year trial because there was limited local support for our efforts.'

Examples abound of the commercial advantages of a business voluntarily taking the lead on corporate responsibility and sustainability. But Maersk Line have found, like many others, that there are limits to this in many situations. Regulatory intervention is needed to secure lasting change and tackle the problem of free-riders. Moreover, enforcement of regulations is vital if those who play by the rules are not to be put at a commercial disadvantage. They point out that the cost of compliance with the 2015 sulphur oxides regulations that are coming into force in Northern Europe and North America require the use of cleaner fuels that are approximately 50% more expensive in so-called Emission Control Areas. The same goes for efforts to tackle corruption and facilitation payments: industry-wide effort is needed if change is to be secured, and Maersk Line is an active member of the Maritime Anti-Corruption Network.

Maersk Line has also found that advantages can accrue to a business that is seen to engage with policy-making positively and transparently. Maersk Line's Sterling explains: 'We support the better regulation of shipping. More regulation is going to happen anyway, such as in relation to sulphur oxides. So, let us make sure it is good law-making – strong enforcement should ensure that the cost of avoidance is higher than the cost of compliance. The benefit of a positive stance is that it gives us credibility, which allows us to shape regulation early in the process.' It will be interesting to see how successful Maersk Line, and partnerships such as SSI, are with their aim of raising standards and enforcement globally – even a partial victory will have significant benefits to air quality and green-collar jobs.

Alliance Boots & the Circular Economy Task Force

'Sometimes, a well-meaning piece of legislation can have far reaching, negative unintended consequences when it comes to advancing sustainability. So a key intervention our Corporate Responsibility team can make is to ensure law-makers understand such policy failure', argues Richard Ellis, Group Head of CSR at Alliance Boots, a pharmacy-led health and beauty group.

In recent years, a large number of businesses have become increasingly concerned about resource scarcity and rising prices. Brent crude was selling at US$16 a barrel in 1993 – it has spent the bulk of the last couple of years priced at over US$105 a barrel. Over the same period, the Commodity Food Price Index has virtually doubled and the Metals Price Index more than tripled. Put simply, human impact on the environment is now exceeding multiple environmental limits. On the plus side, McKinsey have estimated that improvements in resource productivity could meet 30% of global resource demands by 2030 and generate savings in the region of £1.9 trillion.

These pressures led a group of six businesses to join Green Alliance's Circular Economy Task Force in 2012: Alliance Boots, BASF, Interface, Kyocera, Veolia and Viridor. In 2013 they issued a report, *Resource Resilient UK*, which described what businesses and government could do to secure resources for industry through a more circular economy. As one might expect, the Task Force identified how reuse, remanufacturing and secondary material supplies can address the root causes of resource insecurity. However, it also concluded that one of the three areas of action needed to be 'facilitating co-operation'; and, one of the key recommended interventions was therefore that Government needed to clarify 'competition law to reinforce exemptions for environmentally beneficial co-ordination between businesses'.

For a circular economy to emerge there will need to be more collaboration between businesses than there is now, as decisions made at one stage of a product's value chain knock on to the potential for circularity in later stages. Yet, the Task Force concluded that competition law was having a chilling effect on collaboration and this needed to be remedied. Anti-trust or competition law at the local, national and international level is a common instrument by which government inhibits data sharing amongst industry peers to prevent collusion and mal-practice (e.g. price rigging, destroying rivals). Whilst well intentioned, it is vital such laws do not result in an impact that is the opposite of their aim. The Task Force found a culture of fear existed, given such law was open to wide interpretation and potential penalties for breaching it are extremely high. Alliance Boots's Richard Ellis says that: 'Competition law was, for example, inadvertently undermining the implementation of the EU Eco-design Directive and useful data sharing amongst industry peers. This harms our company's goal to design, source and sell more sustainable products. We want to still be around for our 250th anniversary in 2050, and this requires doing business in a smartly regulated marketplace.'

The response of UK and EU lawmakers to this call for change remains outstanding, but the Task Force has certainly done well to bring these unintended consequences to the attention of key influencers.

Lessons in leadership

- When one business seeks to do 'the right thing', do not be surprised if others want to join in – but someone has to make the first move

- With enough support, a business can have a seat at the highest table of policy-making

- The opportunities to Lobby for Good are immense – everything from the local through to the global

- Tackling free-riders and their unearned competitive advantage can be a great motivator

- It is not always about new regulations: sometimes enforcement or refinement of existing regulation is a 'big win'

You do not have to be big to drive change

Co-operative Energy

In 1844 a group of 28 weavers and other tradesmen established a co-operative shop in Rochdale, Lancashire, England; a shop that went on to inspire arguably one of the world's most durable grassroots movements. It sold wholesome food at fair prices – a major development given food of the day was routinely adulterated, with hedge clippings added to tea and chalk to flour. But more significantly, the enterprise was owned and controlled by customer members – and this at a time when not only women, but the vast majority of men were denied 'the vote' and excluded from the democratic process. The establishment of the co-operative store was not just an act of self-help, it was a deeply political statement. Many of the founders were frustrated Chartists who had spent years campaigning, unsuccessfully, for an extension of suffrage – the door of the store was painted Chartist green on the opening night and years earlier the first President, Miles Ashworth, led a group to the bloody demonstration that later became known as the 'Peterloo Massacre'. A great many co-operatives in the UK (and elsewhere) have gone on to become adept at *Lobbying for Good*, from giants such as The Co-operative Group (page 55), through to smaller enterprises such as Midcounties Co-operative.

In 2011, Midcounties (which to date had largely been a retailer of food, pharmacy, travel and funerals in the central counties of England) launched Co-operative Energy and began supplying electricity and gas nationally to customers across England, Scotland and Wales. From the outset, the business committed to fair pricing and pledged that the carbon content of its electricity would remain less than half the national average. Moreover, in addition to general support for renewable energy, it actively sought power from community generation initiatives. But it quickly became apparent to the Chief Executive of Midcounties, Ben Reid, and the General Manager of Co-operative Energy, Ramsay Dunning, that they faced an uphill struggle to acquire customers and build market share given the stranglehold of six big energy firms, who between them controlled 97% of the UK energy supply market and benefited from regulation that had evolved to accommodate their interests. Ben Reid believed that: 'As a Co-operative intervening in a market place it's not just about playing the game, it's not even about winning the game – it's about fundamentally changing the game.' Ramsay Dunning thought that: 'Energy policy needed to be radically overhauled and coal power generation phased out at the earliest opportunity.'

So, in 2013 they brought in outside expertise to help them build their capacity to engage with public policy and regulatory reform. They appointed Up the Ethics to help them quickly build contacts and visibility in what is an extremely crowded area. The ultimate aim was to persuade policy-makers that it was in the UK's interest to break the stranglehold of an unhealthily small number of large incumbents suppliers (who had generally been painfully slow to embrace renewable energy) and legislate for a more indigenous and diverse supply base. Neither Midcounties nor Co-operative Energy had a Government Affairs function, but they did have business leaders who were willing to engage energetically and visibly with politicians. The decision was quickly taken to build profile at the forthcoming round of party conferences by joining in with a pending collaboration with three other businesses who had a vested interest in seeing continued growth in renewable energy. This led to a series of roundtable discussions with politicians and culminated in a report, 'The Economic Benefits of Renewable Energy', launched in the Houses of Parliament in March 2014. Support was additionally provided to support interventions arguing for accelerated growth of community-owned renewables generation in the UK, much as already exists in countries such as Germany and Denmark.

Within 12 months, the UK had a government-sponsored Community Energy Strategy in place and the Secretary of State for Energy and Climate Change and Energy was distancing himself from the 'Big Six' and headlining his annual update with statistics highlighting the growth of smaller energy suppliers and further market reforms that would be pursued to encourage diversification of supply. Fantastic progress: and in parallel, Co-operative Energy enjoyed a wonderful reaction from customers to its politically engaged, ethical offering – with customer numbers growing by 55% to 210,000 in less than 12 months.

Obviously, the lobbying actions of Midcounties and Co-operative Energy were not wholly responsible for such significant developments (the likes of Co-operatives UK had been having wonderful impact for some time), but they certainly contributed. Moreover, to ensure good governance and transparency are entrenched early on, an update on active public policy positions is regularly provided to Midcounties Board, and all major interactions are detailed in their Social Responsibility Report. Pete Westall, General Manager of Co-operative Social Responsibility at

Midcounties found that: 'Committee members and the Board as a whole were not just pleased that our Co-operative Energy business had made such headway in such a small amount of team, but were proud that we were standing up for interventions that would benefit community groups and co-operatives all over the UK.'

Main Street Alliance

2012 was the year that the world woke up to the scale of corporate tax avoidance that was being pursued by multinationals such as Apple and Microsoft, with the issue forced on to front pages of newspaper across the globe. 2013 was then the year that small business began to find its voice, urging governments to ensure that large corporations be required to pay their fair share.

In the United States, the Main Street Alliance (MSA) has been particularly active. This national network of small business coalitions was formed in 2008 to give small business owners a voice in the health reform debate, but has since broadened its focus to work on a range of issues that matter to small businesses and local economies. The MSA, directed by a National Steering Committee of small business leaders from state coalitions, identify issue priorities, establish positions and provide direction and guidance. Tax avoidance by large corporations was a priority issue for them through 2013. They are angry that small businesses currently pay a higher effective tax rate than many large corporations, pointing to research showing that (once net assets pass US$25 million) the bigger the corporation, the lower its effective tax rate, with the largest corporations paying a 'bargain' 15.5% rate – less than half the statutory corporate tax rate of 35%. They point out that: 'Small business owners don't have the resources to hire armies of tax lawyers to dream up and implement creative accounting schemes the way big corporations do. American small business owners that pay their fair share are subsidizing large corporations that dodge their tax responsibility.'

MSA want to see corporate tax reform and an end to practices such as the shifting of profits to offshore tax havens, which they say could net US$600 billion to the Government over the next decade. A key campaign tool was the deployment of polling, which showed that small business owners across the political spectrum supported reforms to require corporations to pay their fair share. More than three-quarters (76%) supported closing offshore tax loopholes by basing corporate taxes on where sales are made, where employees work, and where assets are located; and, by a margin of more than two to one, small business owners prefer closing corporate tax loopholes rather than cutting spending on welfare and infrastructure. They also deployed NGO-style tactics to keep the issue alive: in September 2013 a half-dozen members visited the headquarters of Microsoft to deliver an open letter signed by more than 200 local small business owners. The campaign is making real headway, with two separate bills now introduced by Senators to tackle the abusive use of tax havens.

The rise of social enterprise and B-Corps

Coalitions of mid-corporates and small businesses acting together for the common good are mushrooming on both sides of the Atlantic.

The American Sustainable Business Council (ASBC) was a key partner with Main Street Alliance on their campaign to end offshore tax dodging, and are the organiser of the Fair Minimum Wage campaign (see page 59).

The ASBC was only founded in 2009, but has quickly grown into a national partnership of over 60 business associations representing 200,000 businesses and 325,000 entrepreneurs, managers and investors. Its mission is to 'advance public policies that ensure a vibrant, just and sustainable economy'; and it certainly delivers on this, offering up a range of issues for business to get involved in. An integral part of the strategy is to get business leaders (with the 'right stuff' one assumes) in front of legislators; to which end they secured over 500 meetings in 2013 alone. Key wins included: confirmation of preferential candidates to key administrator positions, such as Gina McCarthy at the EPA; paid sick leave legislation in New York State; as well as progress on an improved minimum wage (page 59).

Another rapidly growing hub of public policy intervention is social enterprises, which are variously defined around the world, but are essentially businesses that trade for a social and/or environmental purpose. A recent manifestation in the United States are B-Corps, of which over 500 have been certified by 20 states as 'a new classification of corporation that voluntarily meets higher standards of corporate purpose, accountability and transparency'; and close to a thousand have been certified by the originator of the idea in 2007, the non-profit B-Lab.

In the UK, there are now more than 70,000 social enterprises, that between them contribute £18.5 billion to the UK economy and employ almost a million people. Ably led by Social Enterprise UK (SEUK), for whom 'political engagement has been the bedrock of work' since it was established in 2002, the sector is enjoying fantastic growth (even during the recent recession) and broad political support. At the last General Election in 2010 they successfully persuaded each of the major political parties to commit to do much more for the social enterprise sector, and subsequently secured a number of legislative gains: the Localism Act 2011, the Health and Social Care Act 2012 and the Public Services (Social Value) Act 2012. And as with the US's ASBC, a network of progressive networks has recently emerged, the Social Economy Alliance. This will act as an umbrella for the likes of SEUK, Co-operatives UK and dozens of others in the run up to the 2015 General Election.

Perhaps finally, the collaboration of progressive business is reaching a stage where it can take on the regressive might of the likes of the UK's Institute of Directors and the US Chamber of Commerce – if so, it really will be a case of 'game on' for the sustainable economy.

Lessons in leadership

- There are plenty of agencies out there who can get you *Lobbying for Good* quickly – those with good links to NGOs might offer added traction

- The media loves a good David versus Goliath story – if you have got it, use it

- Anger is not always the enemy of reason – demons run when a good person goes to war

- There are lots of great networks out there – choosing which one to go with is the hardest bit

- Keep an eye out for emerging super-networks (especially if connected to mega-trends) – they may be the means for game-changers to really make some waves

CHAPTER 3

Developing Your Approach to *Lobbying for Good*

Towards performance excellence

TO MAINSTREAM THE PRACTICE of *Lobbying for Good* requires a systematic rethink of the role of lobbying in corporate responsibility and sustainability strategies.

As shown in Chapter 1, the vast majority of media scrutiny and literature on corporate lobbying has to date focused on the negative behaviour of big business and the need for compensatory measures. Major advances are being made in North America and Europe in relation to lobbying regulation and transparency. This regulation of the worst excesses and hypocrisies is welcome, but it is nowhere near sufficient to get us to the promised land of a more sustainable society. Something much more proactive and involved is desirable.

Businesses of all shapes and size can lobby for good; and, as demonstrated by the case studies in Chapter 2, this is informed by factors as varied as size, wealth, sector, brand positioning, networks, experience, culture, aspiration, policy challenges and regulatory regime.

The pursuit of excellence and construction of a cutting edge *Lobbying for Good* (L4G) Advocacy Strategy is shaped by 'why' and 'what' a business lobbies on (as driven by factors such as corporate responsibility alignment, commercial gain and societal need) and 'how' it delivers on this (based on enablers such as selecting the issue, building the narrative and mobilising resources) – as depicted in Figure 3 and the L4G Performance Excellence Framework™. Aligning and benchmarking a company's approach with this framework for excellence will help guide practitioners at all stages of maturity.

FIGURE 3. L4G Performance Excellence Framework™

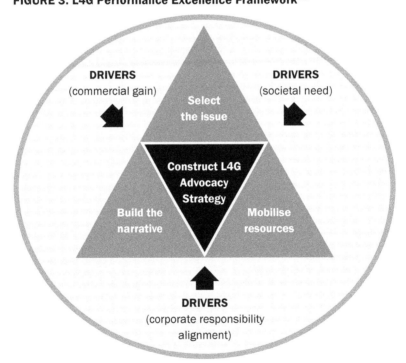

Source: Up the Ethics and Infrangilis, 2014.

Select the issue

Issue selection might initially feel daunting given the vast array of subjects one might seek to act on. As with all major decisions a company makes on policy development or investment, the merits of *Lobbying for Good* need to be compelling. Early ideas can be precipitated and tested via a SWOT analysis (Strengths, Weaknesses, Opportunities and Threats). A strong, independent facilitator will help move matters on more smoothly – especially if this is the first time a business has considered putting its head above the parapet. When conducting such an exercise, one needs to be vigilant for those who view the business through rose-tinted glasses; and will enthusiastically talk up middling performance and talk down the problem of self-evident areas of weakness. Equally, expect there to be people who will see weakness everywhere and use this as an excuse to stymie progress in any area – perhaps question whether such an approach would be allowed to guide other business initiatives. Other factors to be mindful of include:

- Strengths – once the areas have been identified where the business has strong performance and good internal expertise (e.g. energy efficiency or labour standards), drill down further to determine the elements that have driven this

- Weaknesses – it can sometimes be difficult for one colleague to identify another colleague's domain as an area of weakness, so perhaps use external benchmarks to initiate discussion (e.g. Greenpeace's Scorecard on Palm Oil Producers or Oxfam's Behind the Brands Scorecard)

- Opportunities – look for key events taking place 12–18 months hence that may raise the topicality of an issue and open up significant engagement opportunities: this could be anything from a global convention on climate change or biodiversity through to a general election or referendum

- Threats – the economic health of the business (perceived and actual) 12 months down the line should be considered; it might sit uneasily for a business to argue for living wages abroad whilst laying off staff at home

Crucially, whatever issue is landed upon needs to be material and aligned to core business activities. As argued convincingly by AccountAbility in the *Materiality Report* (**http://www.accountability.org/images/content/ 2/0/202.pdf**), however, it is important not to define materiality too narrowly – issues need to be considered in terms of their relevance to:

- short- and long-term financial performance,

- ability to deliver on strategy and policies,

- best practice norms exhibited by peers,

- stakeholder behaviour and concerns, and

- societal norms, particularly where linked to possible future regulation.

Particular attention should be afforded to corporate responsibility and emerging peer-based norms. There may be a number of standards that a company already uses that would benefit from *Lobbying for Good* activities. The current version of the Global Reporting Initiative Sustainability Reporting Guidelines, which is used by more than 6,000 companies worldwide, contains two public policy performance indicators

(SO5 and SO6). The Carbon Disclosure Project, which represents over 700 institutional investors and US$92 trillion of investments, requires disclosure of lobbying activity aligned to climate change in respect of direct engagement with policy-makers, but also indirect influence via trade associations and research bodies (CC2.3a-i).

Getting ahead of the curve on societal need is something of an art form. Over the period 2008–2011, the Co-operative Group was adept at this, identifying areas such as neonicotinoid-induced pollinator decline and the exploitation of unconventional fossil fuels (such as tar sands and gas shales) as big pending issues. This meant it not only brought these issues to the public's attention, but benefitted from significant positive PR as a first mover – in the region of £3 million equivalent advertising value was secured in a single year. The work highlighting the impact of neonics helped instigate a broader set of campaigns that led the European Commission to enforce a temporary ban on their deployment in 2013.

A good way for a business to start getting its head around these issues is to subscribe to information feeds from those who make it their job to track mega-trends and breakthroughs in science and technology. For example, the annual State of the World reports from the Worldwatch Institute, or the periodic United States' National Intelligence Council Global Trends Report. At a national level, many countries have now identified (and report on) sustainable development indicators, and these can often reveal where societal progress is and is not being made. Local authorities and municipalities may even drill down further, and are useful should a business wish to identify and champion an issue at a local level (especially if that business's core products and services relate to urban infrastructure). Those comfortable with scientific literature will find weekly publications such as New Scientist and Nature a treasure trove of ideas, not least in connection with issues such as resource scarcity, as prioritised by the Circular Economy Task Force (page 40).

General Electric and Unilever

Horses for courses – routes to issue selection

Unilever. In 2011, the Advocacy team identified the following as areas where lobbying could make the biggest difference to achieving the ambitious targets in their Sustainable Living Plan:

- influencing greenhouse gas policy to achieve a policy environment which promotes low carbon;

- promoting the importance of washing hands with soap in countries where this issue is not high on the public health agenda;

- improving recycling and waste infrastructures to increase national recycling rates; and,

- enhancing trade policy terms for sustainably sourced agricultural commodities to encourage a more systemic shift towards sustainable agricultural practices.

General Electric. In 2012, the following priorities were identified by the Government Affairs team as part of their standard annual review process:

- intellectual property protection

- free trade

- tax reform

- promotion of exports

- regulations associated with financial services reform and healthcare reform

- advanced propulsion for military aviation

- data-privacy and -protection legislation

- rule of law, globally

- patient safety

- access, quality and cost reforms in healthcare

- access to critical manufacturing materials

- cyber security

- natural gas policy

- advanced manufacturing

- development policy

- global environmental and energy policies.

As discussed in Chapter 2, Unilever's issue selection process is led by its Advocacy team and intimately linked to its Sustainable Living Plan (page 29). However, the more standard route is for this to be co-ordinated by the Public Affairs/Government Relations function. This can often be a weaker pathway to progressive action as it leads to old school practices of the pursuit of self-interest in the narrowest of fashions; although, as shown by General Electric (GE), more and more businesses are now seamlessly integrating the disclosure of their public policy activity with their regime for sustainability reporting. Semi-annually, the GE Government Affairs and Policy team ask each of the company's business teams to provide an assessment of their legislative and regulatory priorities (with links to a GE objective). The businesses also provide input on the appropriate advocacy plan or strategy for achieving a successful outcome, including whether or not GE will advocate for a priority directly or through one of its trade associations or industry coalitions. The Government Affairs team then determine GE's overall public policy priorities taking account of GE's strategic objectives. They point out that ultimately 'there is no pre-assigned formulae for prioritisation'; but tax, trade, rule of law and intellectual property protections are typically top priorities. It's doubtful that all this activity is progressive, particularly the work around tax reform; however, GE deserve credit for allowing the details to emerge into the light of day.

And lastly, when selecting an issue it is important to recognise that some aspects have a natural attention cycle. There is an initial pre-problem stage, which is followed by alarmed discovery and a willingness to respond. Then, when it becomes clear that progress will be a little more difficult than first envisaged, interest cools and a campaign enters a more difficult phase requiring real effort. Things may go quiet for a while, only for the issue to resurface again as a cause for alarm. If such a cycle applies (as happens with subjects that have been around for some time) it is important to be clear in what phase an issue is because it can have a big impact on the ease of engaging an audience.

Build the narrative

Once a compelling issue (or set or issues) has been identified, it is important that a narrative and emotional hook be established between the opportunity/problem and the necessary legislative solution. A motivational story is needed that demonstrates the creation of shared value for the society as well as the company – it may help to build this narrative early so that it can help secure buy-in for the proposal internally.

Vintage Vinyl and ASBC

Sweet music to anyone's ears

The public position of the independent music retailer Vintage Vinyl is that 'the American Dream needs a minimum wage increase', a story syndicated by newswires around the world. Vintage Vinyl is a signatory to the Business for a Fair Minimum Wage campaign, which is supported by the American Sustainable Business Council (page 47).

The coalition of 200,000 businesses says that increasing the minimum from today's US$7.25 to US$10.10 will build a stronger economy. It has produced comprehensive studies to show that increasing the minimum wage, which has been at the same level since 2009, will not negatively impact employment. Just as importantly, it is arguing that raising the minimum wage has strong public support across the political spectrum with 80% of Americans, including 62% of Republican voters, supporting a raise. States such as New Jersey and California have passed ballot measures to unilaterally raise their rates; and President Obama is seeking approval in Congress for a national increase to U$10.10.

When building the narrative, be guided by the three Ss of effective storytelling: the story should be *sharp*, *simple* and *short*. It will need to encompass:

- why the issue is important for society at large (e.g. how aggressive tax avoidance leads to a significant loss of revenue for government welfare programmes);

- how taking a voluntary approach has been tried and failed (e.g. despite public uproar, the tax gap remains as enormous as ever);

- what the company is asking legislators/regulators to do (e.g. close loopholes that tax havens to be used unscrupulously); and

- why taking action can make a huge difference (e.g. the extra revenues could pay for hundreds of thousands of teachers and/ or nurses).

If there is a mass mobilisation element to the initiative, then the narrative should also cover:

- what action the company is asking people to undertake (e.g. sign a petition, contact a Member of Parliament or Congress);

- why it is important to act now (e.g. a general election is approaching and this provides a great opportunity to influence policy formulation);

- compelling images, given 'a picture paints a thousand words' (e.g. infographics); and

- remember that it is much harder to engage people on a broad subject (e.g. social justice) compared to a specific issue (e.g. paying a living wage).

Framing the story is critical to its success. Information needs to be placed into a context that makes it more palatable to a particular group. For example, conservative sceptics will be more accepting of climate science if it is framed as supporting a free-market solution that they find appealing for ideological reasons, such as market investment in nuclear power. Ideological predispositions skew everyone's consideration of facts, and framing can help counter (or exploit!) what is essentially human irrationality.

In recent years there have been major advances in the understanding of the psychology of decision-making. Daniel Kahneman's *Thinking, Fast and Slow* is an excellent summary of the latest research – **explaining, for example, why you are more likely to believe this statement on the basis of it being in bold.** Similarly, the manner in which Richard Thaler and Cass Sunstein have taken these ideas, developing Nudge Theory and applying it to public policy design, is informative – not least because their work is in vogue with governments the world over and can act as a useful engagement tool.

Another factor to bear in mind when developing a narrative is that policy-makers (and to a degree the general public and media) are particularly sensitive to any subject matter that can be reduced to the numbers of jobs created or destroyed in their locality. Environmentalists will often bolster support for greenhouse gas reduction targets and renewable energy by painting a picture of how a green economy might look and the jobs that will be created getting there. But 'jobs lost' will equally be the last refuge of those who have exhausted every other argument to save a product that has been proven to kill or pollute – be it restrictions on the export of jobs to oppressive regimes or the phase out of toxic chemicals.

Mobilise resources

The success of a lobbying initiative is in large part dependent on the resources available. As we saw in Chapter 2, businesses of all sizes have a range of options open to them – from a well established multinational such as Unilever with its in-house Advocacy team through to a young gun new-start like Co-operative Energy and its use of outsourced advocacy advice.

So, an early decision involves the degree to which a business will go it alone or seek to influence with others. There are obvious trade-offs to be made: going it alone carries with it the possibility of significant reputational enhancement, but carries with it greater risk and resource requirements; operating in a coalition will de-risk the venture and likely save on resources, but little bespoke recognition may be realised.

Fortunately, a solution to this dilemma lies in the fact that many collaborative efforts offer tiers of involvement. It is not unusual for there to be four to ten ringleaders in a collaborative campaign: who will kick-start activities, provide seed-corn funding, call the shots and divvy up brand enhancement opportunities. Other businesses will likely have the opportunity to sign-on for little or no cost, but can expect to have little say or visibility. Acting as a leadership company in such a coalition is a useful entry point for businesses who want to learn the ropes of *Lobbying for Good* as they will secure an inside track on the rules of the game. This is particularly true if a business is operating abroad and away from its home base.

Acting as a leadership company should additionally provide an opportunity to work with NGOs, who often lie at the centre of such coalitions. Take the issue of climate change, where: the University of Cambridge Programme for Sustainability Leadership co-ordinates both the Corporate Leaders Group on Climate Change and ClimateWise (page 35); the United Nations drives Caring for Climate; the Climate Group runs the Clean Revolution; and the Coalition for Environmentally Responsible Economies (CERES) is at the centre of Business for Innovative Climate & Energy Policy (BICEP) in the United States (see box). Similarly, with the issue of sustainable urbanisation: the United Nations convenes both the World Urban Campaign and the Global Initiative for Resource Efficient Cities; BioRegional operates One Planet Communities; and the World Economic Forum runs the Future of Urban Development Initiative.

Nike and BICEP

Flexing their muscles

Business for Innovative Climate & Energy Policy (BICEP) was launched in 2008 by CERES with a core group of five companies, including Starbucks, Nike and Levi Strauss & Co. In March 2014, Aveda became the 30th consumer-facing company to join the coalition. BICEP seeks to work with policy-makers to pass meaningful energy and climate legislation to both ensure that the US remains competitive in the global transition to clean energy and that member businesses and communities are sustainable and thrive over the long term. In 2013, the coalition developed an emotive Climate Declaration that calls on American business to 'take a stand and do the right thing'; this has now been signed by over 750 businesses. In their Corporate Responsibility Report, Nike cite their work with BICEP as the primary means by which they have advocated for climate change legislation.

> The world needs the United States government to agree significant and binding greenhouse gas reduction targets. The efforts of BICEP and others will be crucial to building the political consensus that will be necessary for this to happen.

NGOs can also be a great source of talent if a business goes down the route of building an advocacy team. It is not coincidental that leaders in the area have all headhunted influential individuals from the NGO world with a track record of working well with business and politicians. Thomas Lingard (page 30) entered Unilever from Green Alliance, Steve Howard (page 32) joined IKEA from The Climate Group, Aviva's Steve Waygood (page 37) and Maersk Line's Jacob Sterling (page 39) were both recruited from WWF and the author Paul Monaghan learned his trade at the Lloyds and Midland Boycott Campaign before joining the Co-operative Group (page 55).

Regardless of whether you are a big business with lots of in-house expertise or a smaller business with functions outsourced, at the end of the day, it is important to get the biggest 'bang for your buck'. Ideally one would hope to draw upon the competencies of colleagues and suppliers from outside corporate responsibility/sustainability, such as public affairs/government relations, marketing, media relations and legal affairs.

When challenging the status quo, one should expect barriers to arise that slow down or prevent the seeds of change taking root. These obstacles may be internal or external, ranging from defensive colleagues in legal or public affairs for whom highly visible lobbying may be countercultural, through to industry laggards who want to marginalise a new leader that wants to drag the rest of the sector up to its high standard. Even when approval of a public policy intervention has been secured from on high, it is not unusual for colleagues in other departments to be less than supportive. In such circumstances, as with 'Issue Selection' (page 52), an independent facilitator can prove to be a great asset: acting as an honest broker, as well as an issue and process specialist. It might be that early forays into *Lobbying for Good* are limited in scope and do not rely on the support of lots of different colleagues. However, once activity has been pursued and the roof has demonstrably not caved in, then the business of securing real change can commence. Alternatively, consider mobilising a senior business leader to front the issue in public – this will not only help open the doors of external influencers further down the line, but has an amazing capacity to ensure that resources quickly fall into place when needed.

If resources permit, the appointment of a dedicated Advocacy professional is worth considering. They can really add value: monitoring external developments; disseminating information; fielding inquiries; liaising with internal and external partners; drafting and approving copy; ensuring integration with governance and reporting systems; and undertaking impact assessments of progress and outcomes of campaigns. Although be ready for lots of applicants – these roles can prove to be very popular!

Construct the L4G Advocacy Strategy

Once you have selected the issue, built the narrative and mobilised resources you are nearly good to go.

Influencing the influencers is the ultimate aim, but it can take time before you identify the right people, never mind secure access and influence them. For this reason (and a few others), it is recommended that any first attempts at *Lobbying for Good* are undertaken as partners in a coalition, or in partnership with an NGO. Certainly this should be the case if a business is operating abroad and away from its home base – in such circumstances the learning curve will be steep, and a failure to grasp cultural nuances could inadvertently lead to anything from a faux pas to a lobbying scandal.

If you have no dedicated internal capacity then look to an outside agency to use their contacts to get you up and running quickly. As we saw in Chapter 2, even the largest companies see the value of joining forces with like-minded peers, with the odd NGO thrown in to keep everything kosher. Just make sure a formal agreement is in place that outlines specific roles, responsibilities and anticipated benefits.

When you are ready to act more unilaterally the following checklist can be used to flesh out your Advocacy Strategy and get you moving. It can also be used to assess the strategy of any coalition you are involved in, and your role in it.

- **Focus** – define your objective(s) pragmatically, progress will normally take at least six months and it is not uncommon to see success realised over two years or more

- **Sniff the air** – what is the mood of the nation on your issue, are politicians open to dialogue and is this a priority for them, why is this still an outstanding matter, is the issue likely to be the subject of a public ballot in the near future?

- **Home in** – make sure you are targeting the right levers of power, it may be that a piece of national legislation is largely governed elsewhere (e.g. Europe), or that a State legislature has all the power needed to effect meaningful change

- **Agree tactics** – targeted messages will need to be delivered to key influencers; are they likely to respond to one-to-one meetings and scientific analysis, or is it better to open a dialogue with a weighty petition in your back pocket?

- **Friend up** – even if you are not looking for a formal partnership, let relevant NGOs know if you are going to be playing in their back yard; you never know, they may have some key ideas and intelligence that proves to be crucial

- **Diarise** – build a calendar of action of at least 18 months, but remember to pay due regard to the natural cycles of democratic governance (e.g. political recess, budget announcements, elections and manifesto setting)

- **Create razzmatazz** – it is a rare campaign that will not benefit from a bit of theatre and razzmatazz, perhaps connected to a petition hand in or release of poll findings; and it is great for morale and PR

- **Track back** – double check that the resource mobilised and narrative built are fit for purpose, and that you have all the facts and figures you need to carry the day

- **Launch** – in the first cycle you may want to keep things low-key as you learn what is what, but in future years an announcement of intentions is advisable; brand enhancement will be realised and it may precipitate friends and allies out of the ether

- **Be honest with yourself** – evaluate where you are six months down the line and determine what is and is not working. An independent facilitator may be needed; remember, a success has many parents but a failure is usually fatherless

- **Be transparent** – lobbying suffers from an image of secrecy and subterfuge, so make sure that your activities are encompassed by your accounting, auditing and reporting systems, and at the right point you are open about your activities

When executing your Advocacy Strategy there are a number of areas to be particularly mindful of given their ability to help and hinder: mass mobilisation, polling and compliance.

Demonstrating support for your point of view amongst the public or another key group will take you far. It is still rare for a business to mobilise its customers in support of a cause and to do so will carry real impact (and demonstrate your legitimacy). Plus, once they have signed up to take action, you can be sure they have a real affinity with your efforts and are likely to do so again. Remember that you are mobilising people to take action, not educating them into a stupor. Take care though that in building lists of supporters you have observed all the relevant privacy and data protections, or that third parties have. If mobilising large numbers of people directly, anticipate that a small but troublesome number may forget they lent their name in support once a politician responds, especially if there is a time lag. Also remember that although we now live in a digital age where social media and online activist platforms such as Avaaz can make breathtaking campaigning breakthroughs in a matter of days, the vast majority of political decision-makers still value the traditional techniques of letter-writing and face-to-face meetings more highly. They know how much more effort they require.

Woolworths

New sustainability champions

In 2011, the World Economic Forum (WEF) identified rapidly growing South African retailer, Woolworths, as one of 16 'New Sustainability Champions' from emerging markets. They operate a chain of food and clothes stores with US$3.2 billion of revenue; and have an unusual degree of control over their supply chain, with 97% of products own-brand.

WEF highlighted that, as one of the four pillars they have in place to shape the company's 'Good Business Journey', Woolworths seek to influence the South African government to improve agricultural standards, labour market issues and education. Their 2013 Sustainability Report notes the emergence of additional areas of engagement: such as food standards & safety, consumer credit & protection, employment equity & transformation and the green economy. They also articulate work with WWF-SA and the Government's Working for Water Programme, and commitments around support for greenhouse gas emission reduction targets.

That an emerging market business such as Woolworths should be embracing *Lobbying for Good* to such a degree bodes well for the future.

Polling is an invaluable tool – helping you 'sniff the air' and 'create razzmatazz'. Try to remember to commission a data set before commencing any activities so you have a baseline to measure progress against: it may even help with building an emerging narrative or securing internal support – just make sure you are the one who gets to see the first cuts of data as they come in. Polling can be used internally to guide strategy or externally as a means to exert pressure – large sections of the media have an addiction to polling results, particularly if the subject matter is one of current debate. In Chapter 2, we saw how The Main Street Alliance (page 46) used polling adeptly to demonstrate that people of all political persuasions supported their campaign for a clamp down on tax havens. Commissioning a poll of a representative sample of the public can be undertaken for around US$5,000. The trick is to get the independent market research agency to piggy-back your survey questions onto a research company's regular polling exercises. Ideally, being representative affords the ability to drill down to any key demographics (e.g. age, gender, income, locality, etc.). You can expect results a few short weeks after commission, and the agency will usually offer (for an additional fee) to analyse and present the data in a graphic form. You may also want to look at your results through the eyes of a politician, who may be particularly sensitive to the views of swing voters. In an ideal world, your policy ask will sit well with the target electorates that so motivate party political discourse – such as the 'squeezed middle' or 'strivers'. Done correctly, polling is the gift that keeps on giving.

Compliance is increasingly a key consideration in connection with lobbying. As explained in Chapter 1, rules are in place for North America, and are progressing across Europe. In the UK, it seems likely that they will impact NGOs as well. In the US, a large business will typically file quarterly activity reports and bi-annual contribution reports. These can be trip points if not completed with rigour as campaigning journalists and NGOs regularly plough through submissions to look for anomalies, as Ford found early in 2014, when its filings appeared to indicate that it backed speedy completion of the Keystone XL tar sands pipeline when its official position is one of neutrality (they later said their activity merely related to 'monitoring' developments).

Practising what you preach applies to *Lobbying for Good* just as much as with any other aspect of your business – perhaps even more so. Whether it is family and friends, politicians or customers, there is nothing more guaranteed to destroy goodwill and reputation than failure to walk the walk. Key questions to consider include are you and your key suppliers:

- signed up to practitioner codes (e.g. European Code of Conduct for Public Affairs Professionals);

- disclosing all political donations (including ballot measure campaigns and affiliated Political Action Committees);

- disclosing all appropriate lobbying activity (in connection with legal requirements and standards such as the Carbon Disclosure Project);

- signed up to any necessary lobbyist registers, be they mandatory or otherwise (e.g. European Transparency Register).

At the end of the day, expect to make mistakes: the policy-making cycle can be a complex and nuanced beast, and it takes politicians many years to understand it themselves. There may not always be deliberate or orderly steps to how a policy process works so you need to be flexible in your approach. Like the funniest jokes, the best lobbying is about great timing as well as good material. Fortunately, the wheels of government turn slowly, which helps if you need to realign a misfiring Advocacy Strategy.

Finally, remember to keep it positive – no-one wants to be lobbied by a misery guts, no matter how compelling their argument. Problems presented to government must be accompanied by workable solutions. Success will be more likely if government becomes convinced a solution is less risky than ignoring the problem. Problems without solutions are tragedies; problems with solutions that are not being enacted have the making of a scandal.

We are entering a time when the logic of *Lobbying for Good* is so strong that it will override the cultural aversion that rails against it, compelling business to act. Doing your bit does not just put you in the company of some fantastic business leaders down the ages, it puts you on the right side of history. Enjoy.

....

For Product Safety Concerns and Information please contact our EU
representative GPSR@taylorandfrancis.com
Taylor & Francis Verlag GmbH, Kaufingerstraße 24, 80331 München, Germany

www.ingramcontent.com/pod-product-compliance
Ingram Content Group UK Ltd.
Pitfield, Milton Keynes, MK11 3LW, UK
UKHW040927180425
457613UK00011B/285